Leaps of Imagination ©2016 by Alice Cotton and Mary Kogan

All rights reserved. Pages of this book can be reproduced for teaching purposes but the whole book cannot be printed in any form or by any means, electronic or mechanical, including photocopying, recording, or by any information storage and retrieval system now known or here after invented, without written permission from the publisher.

THREE DASHES PUBLICATIONS

threedashespub.com

A poster collection of ten Imagination pages are available at the threedashespub.com store

Dedicated to everyone!

LEAPS OF IMAGINATION

by Alice Cotton
and
Mary Kogen

Three Dashes Publications
threedashespub.com

*Ever think,
"I'm bored. There's nothing to do."
Try this…*

*Take apart an old radio and see what's inside.
Splash in a puddle.
Watch a caterpillar walk across a tree branch.
Look out the car window while someone else is driving
and ride the imaginary horse that is galloping alongside .*

*Hike through the woods and notice the hobbits and elves
that live in the trees and under the rocks.
Shoot hoops in the backyard basketball court and hear the
applause as you win the game.
Plunk around on the strings inside a baby grand piano.*

*And know that when you are alone,
free from all adult agendas,
and have plenty of time to dream,
your creativity will come alive,and
your imagination will soar!*

"Logic will get you from A to B, imagination will get you everywhere."

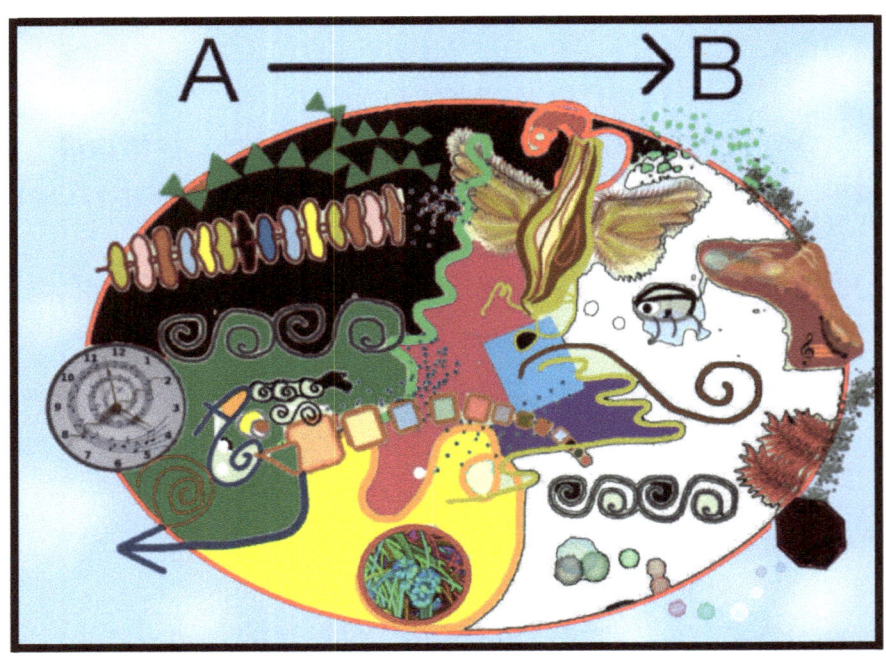

~ Albert Einstein
(1879 - 1955)
German-born theoretical physicist who won worldwide fame for his general theory of relativity and a Nobel Prize in 1921 for his explanation of the phenomenon known as the photoelectric effect.

"Sometimes I've believed as many as
six impossible things
before breakfast."

~ Lewis Carroll
(1832 - 1898)
English writer, mathematician,
logician, author of <u>Alice's Adventures in Wonderland</u> and
<u>Through the Looking-Glass</u>.

*"Without leaps of imagination
or dreaming,
we lose the excitement of possibilities."*

*~ Gloria Steinem
(b.1934)
American feminist, journalist, and social and political
activist, who became nationally recognized as a leader and a
spokeswoman for the feminist movement in the late 1960s and
early 1970s.*

*"If you can dream it,
You can do it."*

*~ Walt Disney
(1901 - 1966)
American animator, entrepreneur, filmmaker, popular
showman, an innovator in animation and theme park design.
He created the characters: Mickey Mouse, Donald Duck,
Goofy, and many more.*

*"Limitations live only in our minds.
But if we use our imaginations,
our possibilities become limitless."*

~ *Jamie Paolinetti*
(b.1964)
American lawyer turned professional bicycle racer.

"Every block of stone has a statue inside it and it is the task of the sculptor to discover it."

~ Michelangelo
(1475 - 1564)
Italian sculptor, painter, architect, poet and engineer. He lived during the Renaissance era and is considered one of the greatest artists of all time.

*"Some stories are true
that never happened."*

*~ Elie Weisel
(b.1928)
Romanian-born Jewish writer, professor, political activist,
Nobel Laureate He was an author of 57 books, including
<u>Night</u>, a work based on his experiences as a prisoner in the
Auschwitz, Buna, and Buchenwald concentration camps.*

"A fool-proof method for sculpting an elephant: first, get a huge block of marble; then you chip away everything that doesn't look like an elephant."

~ Author Unknown

"There are no rules of architecture for a castle in the clouds."

~ G.K. Chesterton
(1874 - 1936)
English writer, lay theologian, poet, philosopher, dramatist, journalist, orator, literary and art critic, biographer, Christian apologist. Chesterton is often referred to as the "prince of paradox."

*"Sometimes imagination pounces;
mostly it sleeps soundly in the corner,
purring."*

~ Terri Guillemets
(b.1973)
U.S. quotation anthologist
Her <u>Quote Garden: A Harvest of Quotations for Word Lovers</u>
is a long-standing online quotation collection located at
www.quotegarden.com.

*"Things are only impossible
until they're not."*

*~ Jean-Luc Picard
The lead character in the TV series
"Star Trek: The Next Generation."
(1987 -1994)*

"Creative people are curious, flexible, persistent, and independent with a tremendous spirit of adventure and a love of play."

~ Henri Matisse
(1869 - 1954)
French artist well known for his paintings, draughtsmanship, printmaking and sculptures.

"The treasures that are hidden inside you are hoping you will say yes."

~ Elizabeth Gilbert
(b.1969)
American author of <u>Big Magic</u>,
and <u>Creative Living Beyond Fear.</u>

"You never have to change anything you got up in the middle of the night to write."

~ *Sam Bellow*
(1915 - 2005)
Canadian-born American writer awarded the Pulitzer Prize, the Nobel Prize for Literature, and the National Medal of Arts.

*"Imagination is the golden-eyed monster
that never sleeps.
It must be fed: it cannot be ignored."*

~ *Patricia A. McKillip*
(b.1948)
*American author of fantasy and science fiction novels, winner
of the World Fantasy Award, the Locus Award, and the
Mythopoeic Award.*

*"Imagination will often carry us to worlds that never were,
but without it we go nowhere."*

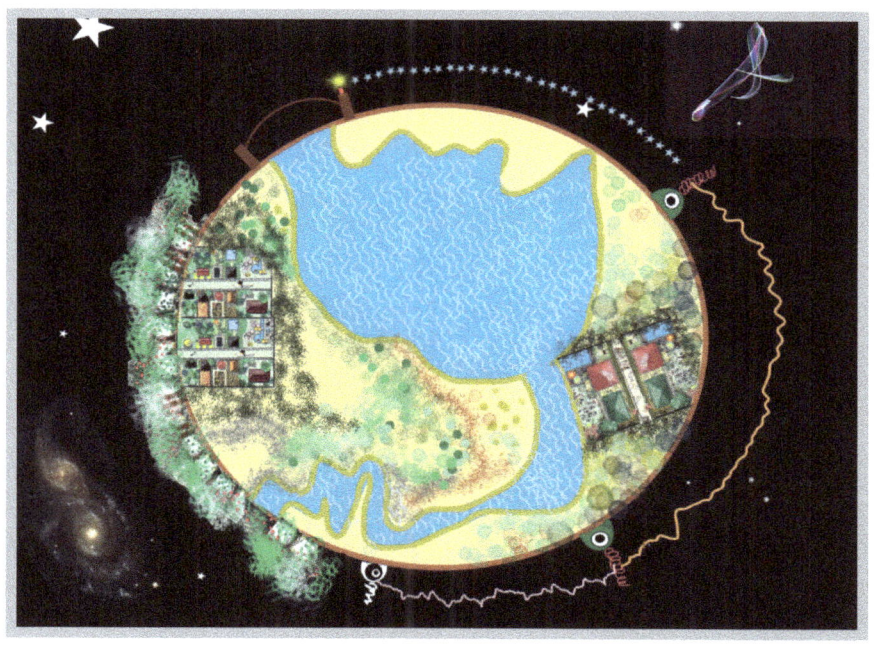

~ Carl Sagan
(1934 - 1996)
American astronomer, cosmologist, astrophysicist, astrobiologist, author, science popularizer, and science communicator in astronomy and other natural sciences.

*"There are several types of chords:
Major, Minor, Augmented
and Demented."*

*~ as told by the grandson of a music class
participant.
(2015)*

"Imagination does not become great until human beings, given the courage and the strength, use it to create."

~ *Maria Montessori*
(1870 - 1952)
Italian physician and educator best known for the philosophy of education that bears her name, and for her writing on scientific pedagogy.

"Imagination is the eye of the soul."

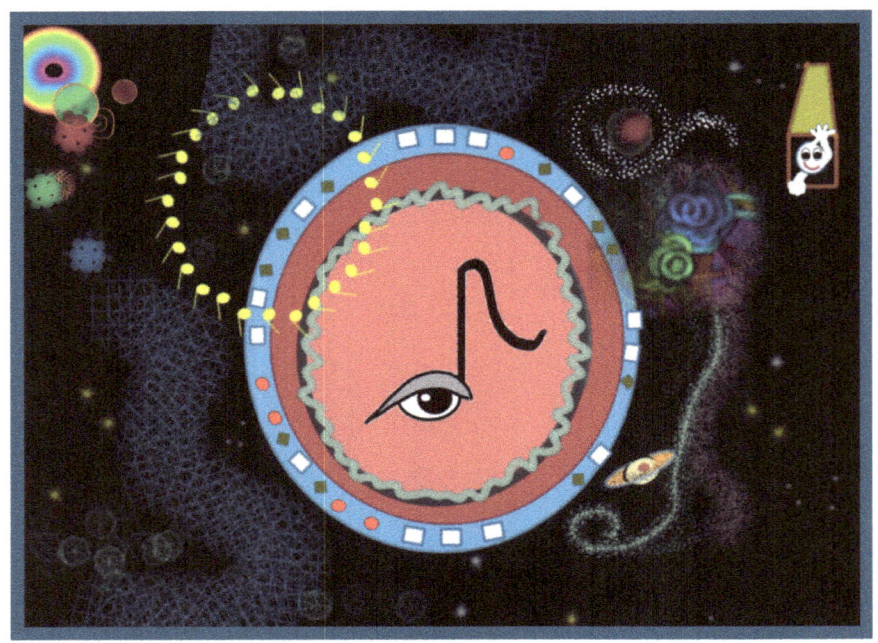

*~ Joseph Joubert
(1754 - 1824)
French moralist and essayist,
remembered largely for his thoughts on the nature of human existence.*

"To invent, you need a good imagination and a pile of junk."

~ Thomas A. Edison
(1847 - 1931)
American inventor who developed many devices including the phonograph, the motion picture camera, and the long-lasting, electric light bulb.

*"Everything
begins with an idea."*

*~ Earl Nightingale
(1921 - 1989)
American radio personality, writer, speaker and author.*

"Live out of your imagination, not your history."

~ *Stephen R. Covey*
(1932 - 2012)
American educator, author, businessman, and keynote speaker. His most popular book was <u>The Seven Habits of Highly Effective People</u>.

"I like nonsense, it wakes up the brain cells. Fantasy is a necessary ingredient in living, it's a way of looking at life through the wrong end of a telescope. Which is what I do, and that enables you to laugh at life's realities."

~ *Dr. Suess (1904 - 1991)*
Full name: Theodor Seuss Geisel
American writer and illustrator best known for authoring some of the most popular children's books of all time.

"Your imagination is the bridge which connects the internal with external experiences."

~ author unknown

"The man who has no imagination has no wings."

~Muhammad Ali
(b.1941)
Professional American boxer and an inspirational and controversial activist.

"Genius is an African who dreams up snow."

~ *Vladimir Nabokov*
(1899 - 1977)
Russian-American novelist known by the pen name Vladimir Sirin. He wrote his first nine novels in Russian, then rose to international prominence as a master English prose stylist.

"The world of reality has its limits; the world of imagination is boundless. "

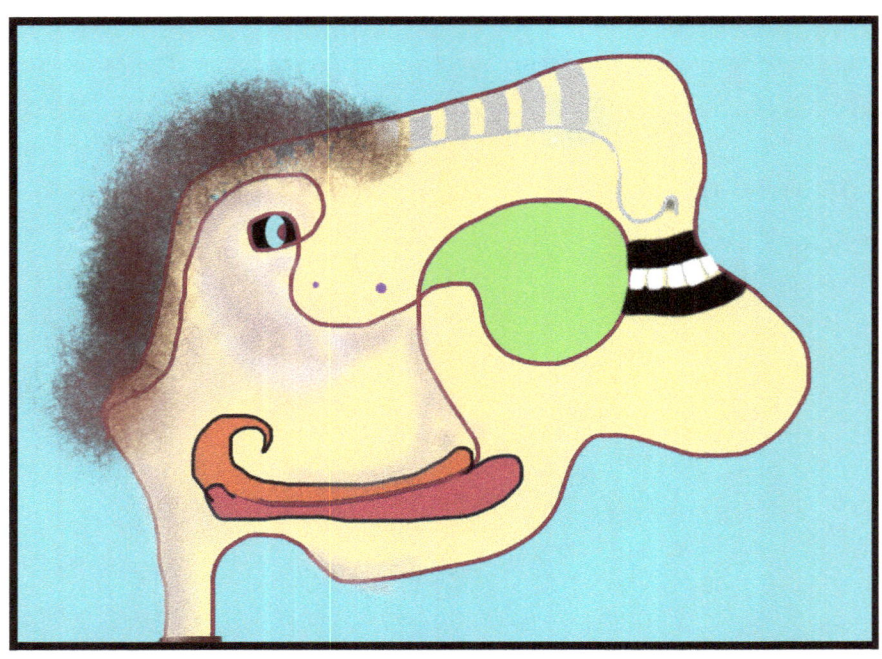

*~ Jean-Jacques Rousseau
(1712 - 1778)
Francophone (French-speaking) Genevan philosopher, writer, and composer of the 18th century. His political philosophy influenced the Enlightenment in France and across Europe, as well as aspects of the French Revolution and the overall development of modern political and educational thought.*

"If you want something in your life you've never had, you'll have to do something, you've never done."

~ Jean Houston
(b.1937)
American author and Mystery School founder which is a New Age self-help or personality transforming program. According to Dr. Houston, "the purpose of the Mystery School is to engender the passion for the "possible." She and her husband are part of the "human potential movement."

"They who dream by day are cognizant of many things which escape those who dream only by night."

~ Edgar Allan Poe
(1809 - 1849)
American writer, editor, and literary critic. Poe is best known for his poetry and short stories, particularly his tales of mystery and the macabre.

"You have many years ahead of you to create the dreams that we can't even imagine dreaming. You have done more for the collective unconscious of this planet than you will ever know."

*~ Steven Spielberg
(b.1946)
American director, producer, screenwriter, a co-founder of DreamWorks Studios, a pioneer of the New Hollywood era and viewed as one of the most popular directors and producers in film history.*

About The Authors

Alice Cotton ~ is an artist, musician, author, and a teacher who continually invites student imagination into all of her classes. She teaches the subjects of mathematics, music, art and architecture, places where imagination can and must flourish.

Mary Kogen ~ holds seminars around the US on learning, curiosity, and play. Using movement, rhythm and sound, she often takes her students on "TaKeTiNa" journeys, which is
a rhythmic process that super-charges student abilities to learn, think, and create.

Together these teachers invite everyone's imagination into their classrooms. What emerges is amazing, surprising and fun. Together they created this book to help inspire everyone's imaginative power.

Alice and Mary also created the book, **Wrong Notes**, where they ask the question: Can mistakes be fun? The answer is "Absolutely!"
Music students, teachers and YOU will love this book!